I0468570

HELP! THE IRS IS AFTER ME!

What Do I Do?

Disclaimer

This book is designed to provide information on tax resolution and taxation only. This information is provided and sold with the knowledge that the publisher and author do not offer any legal or other professional advice. In the case of a need for any such expertise consult with the appropriate professional. This book does not contain all information available on the subject. This book has not been created to be specific to any individual's or organizations' situation or needs. Every effort has been made to make this book as accurate as possible. However, there may be typographical and or content errors. Therefore, this book should serve only as a general guide and not as the ultimate source of subject information. This book contains information that might be dated and is intended only to educate and entertain. The author and publisher shall have no liability or responsibility to any person or entity regarding any loss or damage incurred, or alleged to have incurred, directly or indirectly, by the information contained in this book. You hereby agree to be bound by this disclaimer or you may return this book within the guarantee time period for a full refund.

They disclaim any warranties (expressed or implied), merchantability or fitness for any particular purpose. The author and publisher shall in no event be held liable for any loss or other damages, including, but not limited to, special, incidental, consequential, or other damages.

As always, the advice of a competent legal, tax, accounting or other professional should be sought. The author and publisher do not warrant the performance, effectiveness or applicability of any sites listed in this book. All links are for information purposes only and are not warranted for content, accuracy or any other implied or explicit purpose.

This book contents material protected under International and Federal Copyright Laws and Treaties. Any unauthorized reprint or use of this material is prohibited.

HELP! THE IRS IS AFTER ME!

What Do I Do?

Tips to help you save your job, keep your family, and reclaim your life

By

Vidal Espinosa, MBA

Vidal Espinosa, MBA

ISBN-13: 978-1-5239945-7-1
Arthur Kathleen Publishing
Copyright 2016

Dedication

To my Family who believed in me
and pushed me to follow my crazy Dreams

Contents

About The Author

Vidal Espinosa, MBA has more than 20 years of accounting and taxation experience. Working for large accounting firms such as KPMG and Deloitte, he has a critical eye for substance and quality, strong in budgets, cash forecasts, business, IRS, and Internal Audits. During his time at KPMG providing tax advice to various corporations including being an external CFO for various multinational companies like Sushi ITTO and Sanyo. He is Certified Public Accountant in Mexico from the Universidad Panamericana in Mexico City and CETYS Universidad in Tijuana and holds a Master Degree in International Business by Universidad IBERO-Americana and Business Management Certificate by IPADE Business School in Mexico. As a former professor at Loyola University, he focused on resolving and analyze competitive problems related to the International Markets for Small and Medium Companies.

Introduction

***In this world nothing can be said to be certain,
except death and taxes*** - Benjamin Franklin

Unfortunately, Benjamin Franklin hit the nail on the head. When it comes to dealing with the IRS most people don't want to face the inevitable. Especially when you are faced with a big tax problem. When the IRS comes around to collect, sooner or later you're going to have to face the music. If you play games with the tax collector, the system is designed to make your life miserable. In this country, no one goes to jail for owing taxes. You can go to jail for cheating on your taxes and you can go to jail for trying to trick the tax collector, but you can't go to jail simply because you owe the IRS and can't pay.

Spend an hour with a tax expert before you talk to the IRS. This may be the best hour you've spent in a long time. The expert will tell you how to prepare for your collection interview, how to conduct yourself and make you aware of when the IRS revenue officer is attempting to take advantage of you. You must always remember that the IRS revenue officer's job is to collect money for the Government.

Remember even the IRS agents are human so they personality have good days and bad days. Being kind and compassionate will go a lot way with dealing with the IRS and the individual handling your case. Be honest and fulfill on your commitments to the IRS and a majority of the time things will work out in your favor. You should come to the agent with the attitude that every tax problem has a solution. A good attitude goes a lot way with dealing with your situation and the IRS agent. As the saying goes "You can catch more flies with honey than with vinegar".

How did this happen?

IRS problems are some of the most horrible things you will ever endure. These problems can ruin your health, your work and even sometimes your marriage. First, they can be paralyzing. You ask yourself, what can I do? You're out of answers and you know the problem is getting worse by the day.

Do not allow IRS problems to paralyze you. It helps to know you are not alone and that there are some 800,000 other Americans out there who are unable to pay what the IRS claim they owe. The one way to fight off the fear and paralysis is to get started TODAY. Nothing compounds IRS problems more than doing nothing about them. Every day, the debt will continue to get higher with penalties and interests compounded daily.

First understand: It's not your fault. Life happens.

Unless you promptly get help, this situation will actually get worse, much worse. Interest and penalties continue to accrue against you, plus daily interest on the interest and penalties. IRS problems never go away or get better with age. The irony is that in almost all cases if you had sought help earlier, the IRS problems need not be as big as they usually turn out.

> IRS problems never go away or get better with age, they only get worse

The bottom line is IRS problems can take over your life if you don't do something about it. Once they set the collection efforts in motion, you can no longer handle this behemoth on your own.

Let's look at some of the common events that can lead to IRS Problems:

Unable to Pay Taxes Owed - Many people think, "Oh if I don't file then I won't owe". That couldn't be further from the truth. "It's fine.... I'll just file an extension." No, a tax extension does not give you more time to pay any taxes owed. It only extends the deadline for filing your return! Even if you can pay nothing, you should file on time to avoid a greater tax penalty. You should always file your return on time to minimize your tax penalties. Take a deep breath and try to figure out how much of your tax debt you can actually afford to pay now. You should always pay as much as you can in order to minimize penalties, because your penalties will be based on the amount you still owe to the IRS. Consider these direct tax payment options (which we will talk about later) if you have all or some of the funds to pay the taxes you owe.

Unemployment - If you recently lost your job, the chances are your income has dropped dramatically. That means your tax status has likely changed as well. The loss of a job may create new tax issues. Severance pay, unemployment compensation, payments for any accumulated vacation and/or sick time are taxable. Many people have to dip into their retirement, 401K or equity in their home to make ends meet, thus creating additional tax liabilities that will need to be paid.

Failure to File - Many people don't file taxes for many reasons. "I didn't know they had to", "I didn't make enough money", "My ex-spouse always did it for us", and many others. If you file your tax return

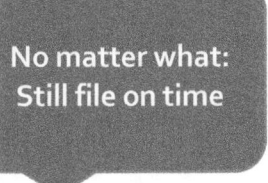

after the deadline, and you did not get an extension, then you will be assessed a penalty of 5% of your balance due per month. The failure-to-file penalty amount will be reduced by the amount you owe for failure-to-pay. The maximum amount you will owe for filing late will be 25% of your unpaid taxes. If you file more than 60 days late, your minimum failure-to-file penalty will be 100% of your unpaid taxes or $135 (whichever is smaller). The IRS will file a return on your behalf and will not take advantage of any exemptions, credits and deductions you are entitled to receive.

Family Issues - This can be one of the most complicated aspects to deal with when it comes to IRS problems. Many ex-spouses are hit with back taxes from their previous spouse. There are three types of relief from joint and several liabilities for spouses who filed joint returns. It is important to discuss with a professional which types of relief which would be best for you to make sure that you are aware if certain conditions to apply. Many times, because of the new status filing as a single taxpayer, they find themselves grossly under withheld and facing a large unexpected balance due to the IRS. This might happen at the same time the taxpayer is starting their new life. Additionally, ex-spouses may withhold tax documents or even not file taxes at all.

Business Problems - As most business owners know, experiencing cash flow problems can be difficult. Many small businesses get into cash flow problems for all kinds of reasons. How they handle these problems, especially when payroll taxes are involved, usually determines if they stay in business or not. Payroll tax problems usually start off with missing one payroll tax deposit and then another and another until you reach the point where you get so scared of how much you owe in missed payroll tax deposits, that you stop filing payroll tax returns altogether. It's not because you want to; it's just that you don't know what else to do. The cash flow problem that caused the shortfall in cash for the payroll tax deposits was most likely caused by any number of factors - all of which are usually outside of your control. Here's where things get really nasty. Not only does your cash flow dry up, but all the customers' goodwill you worked so long and hard to create is now destroyed. Your customers look at you as a deadbeat or tax cheat. They may not say it, but they are probably thinking it.

The IRS will file a substitute return for you

Miscalculations - Everyone makes mistakes, accidently leaves out some income or forget some credit or deductions. When you submit your federal income tax return to the Internal Revenue Service (IRS) each year, obviously the idea is for you to submit an accurate tax return. When the IRS receives your federal income tax return, officials perform several basic checks and reviews of  the information on the return, before accepting the return and beginning to process your refund (assuming a refund is due to you). It is also possible that the IRS will make a mistake when determining your return is not accurate, resulting in a miscalculation of the tax debt you owe. If you believe a mistake was found, it would be a good idea to get a tax professional involved.

The first step in understanding how to free yourself from IRS problems is to appreciate the power of the IRS. There is no question IRS is the most feared governmental agency around. Many powerful men and women have been brought to their knees by the IRS.

Unlike some other problems in life, IRS problems do not get better with time – they are, in fact, almost guaranteed to get worse unless you address them. The majority of the time, believe it or not, the IRS is willing to work with you as long as you're in communication with them. Also, once you talk to a tax professional, you may be able to navigate a way out of the mess faster and better than you had thought.

What can happen?

One of the most unnerving thing is that first letter from the IRS – what do they want? It does not matter whether you're actually liable or guilty; no one wants to hear from the IRS! They are afraid what the letter would say. The conventional sense is that no positive thing can come out of the IRS letter.

If you owe taxes, the IRS will send you a bill. This is your first bill for tax due. Based on your return, they will calculate how much tax you owe, plus any interest and penalties (if applicable). Many clients call a professional with a CP14 in hand. Maybe you forgot, maybe you've put it off, or maybe you never knew you owed additional taxes to the IRS. Regardless of the reason, this notice details what you owe and how long you've had the balance. While it's always best to act early, it's worth getting tax advice should you receive this letter and not know how to proceed.

> **If you don't pay your first bill, the IRS will send you at least one more bill**

So you are not so afraid of what these letters will contain, **Figure 1.1** in the appendix shows what they will look like.

If you still don't pay after you receive your final bill, the IRS will begin collection actions. Collection actions can range from applying your subsequent tax year refunds to tax due (until paid in full) to seizing your property and assets. If you've owed a balance to the IRS that you haven't paid, they'll eventually attempt to seize funds from any legitimate source of income.

The CP504, or more recently the LT-11 and LT-16 letters - while intimidating - are still fairly early in the collection process and let's a professional know that the collection process has begun. If you did nothing after getting these letters, you would probably receive a levy on bank accounts or wages in about 90 days.

Remember, interest and penalties continue to accrue until you've paid your full amount due. See **Figure 1.2**

You already received a CP-504 OR LT-11 letter and haven't taken action, and now the IRS is reminding you of its intent to levy - this time they mean business. If you don't respond in 45 days, you can expect a bank levy or wage levy. The 1058 letter usually comes from a Revenue officer. The equivalent of this letter in Automated Collection Systems is not numbered and just says FINAL NOTICE OF INTENT TO LEVY.

Figure 1.3 shows the type of letter to expect.

> **It is at this point you need to get a professional involved**

The IRS warned you twice, and now your wages/salary are being levied. This means a legal seizure (or levy) of property or rights to property to satisfy a tax debt. When property is seized ("levied"), it will be sold to help pay your tax debt. If wages or bank accounts are seized, the money will be applied to your tax debt. It's not too late to take action at this point, but you'll want to act quickly and attempt to release the levy.

Figure 1.4 shows a letter of the final levies on your account.

Many people are so scared to open the notices - they just hand all the envelopes to their hired professional. This is the worst thing you can do. IRS problems can be scary, but the solution is not to ignore them. The IRS is willing to work with you as long as you are in contact with them.

The good news is that help is available – and the sooner the better. The sooner a tax professional gets involved in helping resolve your tax problem, the better the chances for a prompt and effective solution. With the assistance of a seasoned tax professional, you may engage the IRS by being current and filing all your back taxes, and establish the actual extent of your debts.

Communication is key with the IRS!

Should I hire a professional to resolve my IRS problems?

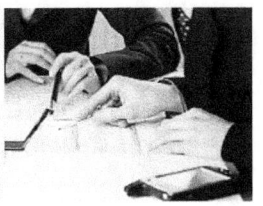

Sometimes, taxpayers with IRS tax problems decide to face the IRS on their own. Sometimes they hire a professional like a CPA, Attorney or EA, but not someone who specializes in tax resolution. The best thing to do when faced with an IRS Problem is to hire an expert in tax resolution so you can get the best result possible.

Even if you owe $10,000 or less, have all your income tax returns filed, and are able to pay the amount due over 36 months with a guaranteed a monthly Installment Agreement (payment plan), it's good to pay a small fee to have a professional set it up for you.

Here are the top 4 reasons why hiring a CPA, Attorney or EA is the smart thing to do if you OWE money to the IRS -

1. Contrary to popular belief, you DO have rights as a taxpayer you probably don't even know exists. One of those rights is the right to representation. If an IRS revenue officer or revenue agent calls or "visits" you, did you know you are under no obligation to answer any of their (very intrusive and condescending) questions? You politely respond by asking for their contact information and telling them you are in the process of hiring a professional to represent you and that this person will contact them directly. A CPA or EA that

> A tax resolution specialist will try and get you the lowest possible settlement

deals with IRS problems for a living knows the "ins" and "outs" and how to deal with the IRS so that your rights are protected. Generally, our clients never meet or speak with the IRS once we're on the scene!

2. If you owe between $10,000 and $200,000 plus, the IRS has many NEW flexible programs available to taxpayers such as Offer in Compromise, Partial Pay Installment Agreements, Payment Plans, Penalty Reduction, and Currently Not Collectible Status to name a few. Each carries with it its own unique process, procedures and qualifications.

> Having an experienced Tax Pro in your corner ensures you are taking advantage of the best options

3. Having unfiled returns (on average our clients have more than 3 years of unfiled returns) qualifies for getting professional help. Not filing legally required tax returns when due is considered a federal misdemeanor which carries with it a $10,000 fine and potential jail time. Generally, the IRS won't throw you in jail unless the taxpayer is deemed to owe a lot of money and is uncooperative about getting the returns filed. Hiring a professional to represent you is the smartest move you can make here!

4. If you are being audited or about to be - The IRS will ask you about 50 very intrusive questions in the initial interview with them. How you answer these questions will dictate the fate of your case. Having a tax resolution specialist conduct these meetings, WITHOUT you is the

best course of action I can recommend. Half of the referrals to the IRS's criminal investigation division (CID) come from that "nice" guy or gal your sitting across the table from at the audit.

One last thing...ask yourself this question; Would you go to court without a lawyer? If you answered "yes" hopefully you know the law inside and out concerning your case, but if representing yourself doesn't seem like a good idea, it's best to hire somebody who is well versed in the subject matter. Well, it's the same thing with the IRS. Having someone who knows how to negotiate and deal with the IRS may be the best money you'll ever spend!

Who can help you?

When you first start to tackle the issue of tax problems you must determine who would be best suited to help your situation. Here is a chart of when it would benefit you to get a professional preparer involved:

Issue	
Under $10,000 in tax debt	No
Over $10,000 in tax debt	Yes
If you have not filed taxes within the last year	Yes
Failed on Payments to the IRS	Yes
Unable to make payments to the IRS	Yes

Yourself

The first thing you should know is that if you owe under $10,000 we recommend you handle the situation yourself. There are many free resources that you can get information on how to work with the IRS. Remember if you are in honest communication with the IRS they will help you. Additionally, the Taxpayer Bill of Rights on the IRS website provides taxpayers a set of fundamental rights they should be aware of when dealing with the IRS. Explore your rights and your obligations to protect yourself.

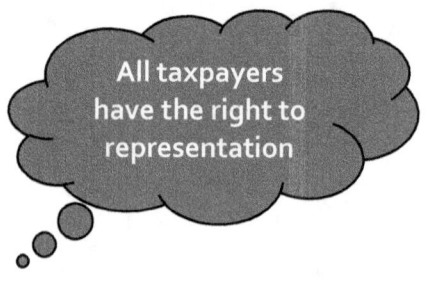

All taxpayers have the right to representation

CPA

A CPA (Certified Public Accountant) will have passed the Uniform Certified Public Accountant Examination and will have met additional state education and experience requirements for membership in their respective professional accounting bodies and certification as a CPA. The advantages to having a CPA is that they have experience in financial and tax matters, however the disadvantage is that they may not be able to competently defend you in taxpayer representation.

Tax Attorney

A tax advisor, or consultant, is a financial expert specially trained in tax law. Working as a lawyer involves the practical application of abstract legal theories and knowledge to solve specific individualized problems, or to advance the interests of those who hire lawyers to perform legal services. The advantages to having a Tax Attorney is that they have experience in legal matters, and the disadvantage is that they may not possess enough knowledge about taxes and the creativity that comes with it.

Enrolled Agent

An enrolled agent (or EA) is a federally authorized tax practitioner empowered by the U.S. Department of the Treasury to represent taxpayers before the Internal Revenue Service (IRS). Just because an EA knows about taxes, this may not give them the ability to defend you in front of the IRS.

Any professional you choose to work with should have experience and credentials in IRS Tax Problem Solving. Select a practitioner with whom you can meet face to face and someone with whom you are comfortable with as you will be sharing a lot of person information with them.

With the assistance of a seasoned tax professional, you may engage the IRS by being current and filing all your back taxes, and establish the actual extent of your debts. Your tax representative may then possibly negotiate a reduction of your debts and arrange for an installment agreement or an Offer-in-Compromise.

How do I find someone?

When you're facing back taxes and you are hounded by the IRS, paying for a tax resolution specialist may seem like an unnecessary cost. In fact, the opposite is true. In those difficult times, retaining a knowledgeable and reliable tax resolution specialist will often result in more affordable IRS payment plans and lesser tax penalties. Failure to hire a professional may be saving a dime while wasting a dollar. In certain instances, the tax payer's cost of hiring a professional is zero because the amount usually paid to the IRS goes to the professional. Tax resolution specialist utilize their specialized knowledge of the tax system and the IRS to get you the tax relief you deserve.

It is no surprise that issues with back taxes and other IRS problems can be both financially and personally crippling. When you hire a professional resolution specialist to assist you with your back taxes, you're also investing in your own piece of mind. As soon as you retain their services, they take over all communication with the IRS. A tax resolution specialist will make sure your tax problem gets the maximum tax relief from start to finish. Here are some places to find a practitioner:

- Invictus Advisors (www.invictus-advisors.com) – Invictus Advisors strives to become knowledgeable in every aspect of a tax situation and provides their clients with quality service in a timely basis. During the process they give clients updates and while offering a comfortable environment to give them the support they need.

- American Society of Tax Problem Solvers – The American Society of Tax Problem Solvers (ASTPS) is a national non-profit membership association that was founded in 2003 to address the needs of a special group of professionals. The Society is comprised of Attorneys, CPAs, and Enrolled Agents who regularly deal with clients suffering from IRS problems.

- Taxpayer Assistance Centers – IRS Taxpayer Assistance Centers (TACs) are your source for personal tax help when you believe your tax issue cannot be handled online or by phone, and you want face-to-face tax assistance. You will be dealing directly with the IRS.

- Taxpayer Advocate Service – TAS is an independent organization within the Internal Revenue Service (IRS). Their job is to ensure that every taxpayer is treated fairly and that you know and understand your rights. If you are having a tax problem that you haven't been able to resolve on your own, our Advocates may be able to help. You may be eligible for our help if your IRS problem is causing financial difficulty, or you believe an IRS procedure just isn't working as it should.

- Research – You can turn to the internet and find a multitude of tax resolution companies. Many of them offer "cents on the dollar" for your case. Be diligent and ask a lot of questions before you sign anything.

There are many companies but not all of them are good like Invictus Advisors

Choosing a reliable and reputable tax relief company is a daunting task. The reality is that many tax problems are better handled and resolved with a tax professional who knows what they are doing. Knowing what questions to ask and what red flags to look for can greatly increase your chances of hiring the right company for you and avoid a scam.

To help you here are 10 tips on How to Hire a Tax Resolution Company You Can Trust:

1. Be wary of demands that the company be paid in full upfront - trust is a two-way street. If you can trust that the company will provide the services as promised in their agreement, they in turn must trust that you will pay them and begin working 100% for you upon receiving a "good faith" retainer.

2. Ask for the names of the owners of the company - any hesitation by their representatives is a definite cautionary red flag that they don't want you to know who is behind the company, and ultimately responsible for your case. Ask to speak with the principles of the firm, they should be more than happy to talk to you. Additionally, call the company, and ask to speak directly to the person who would be assigned your case. Ask about previous cases that they have worked on and their results. Enquire about the way forward where your case is concerned as well as the possible outcomes. A professional who is unavailable or unable to talk to you is a red flag.

3. What is the firm's success rate? As a rule, the firm's track record is the best objective indicator of how that firm

will manage your case. How many Offers in Compromise has the firm successfully settled? What is the total dollars negotiated in settlements divided by total dollars in tax, interest and penalties owed?

4. How long has your company been in business? Most new companies (no matter what the business is) never succeed due to a wide variety of reasons. In today's difficult financial climate, you don't want to get stuck with a company that hasn't been in business for at least three to five years. Otherwise, they might not even be in business six months from now.

5. Do not feel pressured to hire the company. - If it feels like representatives are deliberately trying to scare, intimidate, or otherwise coerce you into hiring them, you will probably regret doing so. Remember, the tax debt resolution professionals you hire will be working for you!

> You should choose someone who is attentive to your needs, and makes you feel comfortable.

6. Research the Company. Are they a member of the American Society of Tax Problem Solvers? Do they have testimonials? Additionally, the credentials should be substantiated by an independent third party, like the Better Business Bureau. You can also ask the firm if they have been designated a Certified Tax Resolution Specialist.

7. Does the firm guarantee results? No firm, up front, can guarantee a result. You must at least see a verified financial statement before rendering an opinion. If the firm is pushing they can get you a tax settlement, leave quickly. The offer in compromise "pennies on a dollar" ploy has scammed thousands of taxpayers. Do not be a fooled.

8. Does the company have flat fees? Most flat fees are contingent upon something, whether it be your participation or on a set amount of days spent on your case. This isn't completely unreasonable, but some companies say one thing and do the exact opposite. Be sure to read a firm's contract carefully. Some firms verbally promise flat fees, but their contracts clearly outline hourly rates. A flat fee can be a good thing, because it encourages your tax professional to work hard to resolve your tax debt. Hourly fees or continuous monthly fees can be dangerous because they don't encourage resolution, but rather unnecessary work and stalling tactics to bill more hours and take more time.

9. Are they a member of the American Society of Tax Problem Solvers? This organization provides their members up-to-date information on continuing education in the field of Tax Problem Resolution. ASTPS is dedicated to providing the best tax resolution education for practitioners.

10. Make sure you need one – many tax resolution companies offer a free consultation. This is where you need to explain your entire situation to a tax professional to see what they can do for you. It is

difficult for a tax resolution company to determine whether or not they can help you until they understand your unique circumstances. Most reputable places will let you know if you can do it on your own.

The good news is that help is available – and the sooner the better. The sooner a tax professional gets involved in helping resolve your tax problem, the better the chances for a prompt and effective solution. Pick a solid, transparent tax debt relief company, and you'll be one step closer to living debt free.

> Educating yourself about your options almost always leads to better decision making - Don't let scammers waste your time and take your money.

Is This the Right Company for Me?

When you sit down with a potential tax resolution company hiring the right tax professional - whether it's a tax lawyer, certified public account or certified tax resolution firm - is vital to your survival against an IRS audit or tax problem. Here is a checklist of questions you will want to ask a tax attorney or tax resolution specialist to ensure you get the IRS tax help you need.

1. Where did this tax attorney or CPA go to school for tax resolution? How current are they (how much continuing education is this tax attorney taking)?

2. How long has this tax attorney or tax professional practiced tax resolution, not straight tax law but real battles with the IRS for tax resolution?

3. What percentage of their jobs are tax problems like yours?

4. Who is their direct supervisor? What is their contact information?

5. Does the individual tax attorney, CPA or tax resolution specialist have references?

6. What is his/her personal success rate? (How many Offers in Compromise settlements have been accepted and what was the negotiated amount owed versus the initial amount of taxes owed and penalties? In short, how much has this individual tax attorney or tax resolution professional saved clients? How does this tax attorney or tax resolution specialist compare to the rest of the firm; above average or below?)

7.   What sorts of releases for tax liens, levies, etc. have they achieved? How fast?

8.   What sorts of penalties (like mine) has this tax attorney/ tax resolution specialist got waived?

9.   What sorts of installment agreements in situations like mine has this tax attorney or tax resolution professional negotiated, and what was the payment schedule?

Since the tax resolution process is not an easy one, you will be working with this firm for a while. Make sure that it is a right fit for them and for you!

This a job interview – Be the Boss!

How can you be helped?

If you are one of thousands of taxpayers dealing with the IRS collection you may feel like there is no relief. The good news is the IRS has many other options available to alleviate an individual's back taxes. Many avenues of Tax Resolution Services exist in the Internal Revenue Code. Knowing which Tax Resolution Services options are for particular situations, and the precedent at the IRS for such situations, is crucial if you want success in pursuing Tax Resolution Services. The following avenues of Tax Resolution Services are the most "known", but are not the only alternatives available.

Having a good Tax Professional is your best bet with the IRS

1. **Offer in Compromise** - An Offer in Compromise allows you to settle your tax debt for less than the full amount you owe. It may be a legitimate option if you can't pay your full tax liability, or doing so creates a financial hardship. The IRS considers your unique set of facts and circumstances including:

    - Ability to pay
    - Income
    - Expenses
    - Asset equity

    They generally approve an Offer in Compromise when the amount offered represents the most we can expect to collect within a reasonable period of time. Explore all other payment options before submitting an Offer in Compromise. The Offer in Compromise program is not for everyone. You must make sure you are eligible.

2. **Installment Plans** - If you're financially unable to pay your tax debt immediately, you can make monthly payments through an installment agreement. As long as you pay your tax debt in full, you can reduce or eliminate your payment of penalties or interest, and avoid the fee associated with setting up the agreement.

3. **Partial Payments Installment Agreement** - The IRS implemented an additional payment option, known as the Partial Payment Installment Agreement (PPIA) for taxpayers who have outstanding federal tax liabilities. Taxpayers who are being considered for a PPIA must provide complete and accurate financial information that will be reviewed and verified. Taxpayers will also be required to address equity in assets that can be utilized to reduce or fully pay the amount of the outstanding liability. In addition, taxpayers granted PPIAs will be subject to a subsequent financial review every two years. As a result of this review, the amount of the installment payments could increase or the agreement could be terminated, if the taxpayer's financial condition improves.

4. **Abatement** - The IRS may provide administrative relief from a penalty that would otherwise be applicable under its First Time Penalty Abatement policy. You may qualify for administrative relief from penalties for failing to file a tax return, pay on time, and/or to deposit taxes when due under the Service's First Time Penalty Abatement policy if the following are true:

- You filed all currently required returns or filed an extension of time to file
- You have paid, or arranged to pay, any tax due
- You didn't previously have to file a return or you have no penalties for the three tax years prior to the tax year in which you received a penalty

5. **Currently Not Collectible** - If the IRS determines that you cannot pay any of your tax debt, they may report your account Currently Not Collectible and temporarily delay collection until your financial condition improves. Being Currently Not Collectible does not mean the debt goes away, it means the IRS has determined you cannot afford to pay the debt at this time. You should know that if we do delay collecting from you, your debt will increase because penalties and interest are charged until you pay the full amount. Furthermore, it is possible for the Statue of Limitations on collection to run out while you are in Currently Not Collectible status.

6. **Statute of Limitations** - In most cases, the Statute of Limitations for the IRS to collect back taxes is 10 years after the IRS has assessed of a tax liability. Essentially, this means the IRS has a 10-year window to collect on a taxpayer's deficiency, and once that window closes the IRS loses its legal claim towards the back taxes. Another important aspect is to avoid triggering the various exceptions to the 10-year Statute of Limitations, which would extend the 10-year period. Common exceptions to be aware of are filing a tax return past the due date, filing an OIC, and filing for bankruptcy.

7. **Bankruptcy** - Contrary to popular belief, filing for bankruptcy will not discharge all tax debt. As a general rule, the income tax at issue must be from returns that were due at least three years before bankruptcy is filed, assuming the returns were filed within the following year and the tax was assessed soon thereafter.

8. **Innocent Spouse** - There are three types of relief from joint debts and several liabilities for spouses who filed joint returns:

   ➢ **Innocent Spouse Relief** provides you with relief from additional tax you owe if your spouse or former spouse failed to report income, reported income improperly or claimed improper deductions or credits.

   ➢ **Separation of Liability Relief** provides for the allocation of additional tax owed between you and your former spouse or your current spouse from whom you are separated when an item was not reported properly on a joint return. The tax allocated to you is the amount for which you are responsible.

   ➢ **Equitable Relief** may apply when you do not qualify for Innocent Spouse Relief or Separation of Liability Relief for something not reported properly on a joint return and generally attributable to your spouse. You may also qualify for equitable relief if the amount of tax reported is correct on your joint return but the tax was not paid with the return.

The most important thing to understand is that we must first determine and fix the problem that caused the tax issue. There can be no lasting resolution until a taxpayer had filed all tax returns and is making current tax payments.

Be honest with your tax professional, they will give the best advice they can!

Is this you?

Many people don't know when they should hire a tax resolution professional. Here are some examples of when you DEFINITELY should:

➤ *Situation: I was worried that I would have to pay taxes so I haven't filed taxes in many years.*
- o Regardless of your reason for not filing a required return, file your tax return as soon as possible. Your tax professional will file the all the returns together and determine what the total tax liability is, if there is any at all.

➤ *Situation: I calculated by taxes and did my tax return but I didn't file it since I can't afford the tax liability.*
- o Don't panic. If you cannot pay the full amount of taxes you owe, you should still file your return by the deadline and pay as much as you can to avoid penalties and interest. There is a penalty for late filing of 5% of the tax not paid by the due date for each month, or part of a month, that your return is late. Generally, the maximum penalty is 25%. Your tax professional can work with you and the IRS on many different payment arrangements, just make sure you file your return.

> It is usually more expensive to file and not pay; then not to file at all.

> *Situation: My spouse and I got a divorce this year and they owed money to the IRS, now I am getting their bills.*
> - There is a way out for some. Under certain circumstances, the IRS provides Innocent Spouse Relief, Separation of Liability Relief or Equitable Relief to spouses who didn't know their exes tax problems BUT there are stringent restrictions. If you think you qualify, talk to your tax professional right away.

> *Situation: I owed money to the IRS and lost my job.*
> - The IRS may be able to provide some relief such as a short-term extension to pay, an installment agreement or an Offer in Compromise, or by temporarily delaying collection by reporting your account as Currently Not Collectible until you are able to pay. In some cases, the agency may be able to waive penalties. If you are already making payments and lost your job, your best option is to contact a tax professional to see what other options are available to you.

> Usually your tax professional can ask for a one-time penalty abatement if you haven't asked for one before

> *Situation: I have received multiple notices from the IRS and haven't open any of the envelopes.*
> - THEY ARE JUST ENVELOPES! An IRS agent is not going to jump out of it, the IRS is not going to know you opened it, and there are no IRS electronic tracking devices in them. Open them and see what they are. They may not be as bad as you think. Who knows, they may even say you have a refund coming to you. One hint: Make sure you keep all of them and bring them to your free consultation with a tax professional.

- ➢ **Situation: I used my payroll tax money to keep my business going; now have no money to pay the IRS for payroll taxes.**
  - o It's easy for cash-strapped companies to give in to the lure of using payroll tax money to keep the lights on. But don't - Uncle Sam does not take it lightly if you don't hand over the money you've taken out of employees' pay. See if you can get a credit line from you bank. If you are unable, there are some non-profit organizations which do small business lending for short periods at higher rates of interest.

    > If you are unable to get lending - contact your tax resolution professional

- ➢ **Situation: My paycheck is going to the IRS and I need to feed my family.**
  - o The IRS is kinder and gentler these days. The agency provides a guide for employers to use to calculate how much is exempt from levy. The amount is based on 1040 filing status and number of dependents, and pay cycle. The difference between net and the exempt amount is sent to the IRS. If you believe that the employer is holding too much or you need a review of your wage levy (or even possibility get it released) contact your tax resolution specialist.

- ➢ **Situation: I just filed for Bankruptcy and can't pay the IRS.**
  - o The Bankruptcy Code requires chapter 13 debtors to file all required tax returns for tax periods ending within 4 years of the debtor's bankruptcy filing. All such federal

tax returns must be filed with the IRS before the date first set for the first meeting of creditors. In reality, only certain income tax is capable of being discharged through bankruptcy. A tax resolution specialist will know which taxes are eligible for bankruptcy discharge.

➤ **Situation: I didn't receive a tax refund from the IRS I was supposed to get.**

   o Visit www.irs.gov/Refunds to check the status of your refund. If the IRS has levied the refund due to back taxes, you would want to contact a tax resolution specialist for them to find out what happened. It could be a variety of reasons including back taxes owed, tax fraud, or miscalculations.

   Make arrangements with the IRS to resolve your tax debt

➤ **Situation: I have no idea how much I owe the IRS and am scared to find out.**

   o Most tax professionals are able to get transcripts from the IRS pretty quickly so be honest with them on how much you owe. They are willing to help you as much as you are willing to help yourself.

➤ **Situation: I tried to use my debt card and I know there was money in my bank account. I contacted my bank and they told me the IRS froze my bank account.**

   o Contact a tax professional right away! In many cases, the levy can be released pretty quickly by your tax professional. What if the levy is producing a financial hardship? An economic hardship occurs when the IRS has determined the levy prevents you from meeting basic, reasonable living expenses. In order for the IRS to determine if a levy is causing hardship, the IRS will usually need you to provide financial information so be prepared to provide it when your tax professional calls. The release of a levy does not mean you don't have to pay the balance due.

➢ *Situation: There was a knock at my door and there was an IRS agent standing there.*
   o First of all, make sure they are with the IRS by asking to see the individual's credentials. Then tell the agent as little as possible, but do not lie, and let them know you will be contacting your tax professional. As soon as you tell an agent that you wish to first consult with a representative, he or she should suspend the interview. Make sure not let the agent into non-public areas and do not give the agent business records or other documents without a warrant. Contact your tax professional as soon as they leave!

Some of the best advice is to be TOTALLY honest with the IRS and your tax professional. They will work with you as long as you are honest and dependable with them. Make sure you actually FOLLOW the advice of your tax professional, get them the documents they request in a timely manner, and be patient!

Make sure you follow the advice of your tax professional

What Do I Need to Do?

The laws have changed over the years—there are laws to protect taxpayers nowadays. Years ago you were just at the mercy of the IRS. But now you have a chance to get your life back. You could opt to represent yourself before the IRS. There is the Offer in Compromise program. Some people do go down that route. But representing yourself before the IRS is like going to court without a lawyer. We wouldn't recommend that.

Or, you can hire someone that knows all the ins-and-outs and navigates the IRS maze on a daily basis. You can hire someone who knows how to protect you and your rights.

> Invictus Advisors are experts in tax resolution

Once you take that first big step and decide you are done with sleepless nights, you need to make the second biggest decision - Hire a competent professional who cares about you and is an expert taking on the IRS.

The only professionals that can represent you before the IRS are Attorneys, CPA's, and Enrolled Agents. That's it! Those are THE ONLY PEOPLE on the planet the IRS recognizes that can represent you. Just like a medical doctor is the only person who can prescribe you medication if you are sick, only Attorneys, CPAs and Enrolled Agents can represent a taxpayer before the IRS. But would you have any doctor prescribe you medication? Would you go to the dermatologist if you had a heart problem? Of course not.

Now what?

There are ways to end IRS Problems, but *you* must decide to end them. When you decide that enough is enough and you want to have the things that everyone has and you're really ready to do something about your IRS Problems, Invictus Advisors can help you.

Once Invictus Advisors is on your case you get immediate relief. We immediately send the IRS a Power of Attorney and the harassment stops. This puts the IRS on notice that you are serious about getting your problems behind you.

> The IRS must now legally deal with them, not you

Additionally, they will:

Stop Enforced Collection Tactics - If the IRS has already started enforced collection activity against you, such as a lien or levy, we will immediately intervene. We file the appropriate documents. In most cases a grace period is granted to work out a more effective course of action.

Provide Professional Evaluation and Preparation - Once you provide us with all the requested information, we carefully prepare the appropriate resolution filings. Depending on the agreed upon strategy, these may include Request for Penalty Abatement, Prior Year Tax Returns, Offer in Compromise, Installment Agreement, Amended Returns, Appeals Request, Application for Innocent or Injured Spouse Relief, Freedom of Information Requests, and so forth.

Handle All Negotiations and Correspondence – In many cases you may have to wait months for the IRS to review and decide on the proposed solution. On occasions, the filing may be rejected for any number of reasons, valid or otherwise. We remove the perceived obstacles and re-file. Because information is required to be current, the IRS may ask that you file and re-file again and again. We request updated supporting documents from you and prepare revisions as necessary. This can be a long and tedious process. The IRS may be backlogged or simply trying to wear you down and hope you give up. You must be patient. When the IRS is ready to finalize your case, the negotiations begin. We do so either by telephone or in person to get you the best possible settlement. Of course, you must approve any final agreement. If your problem cannot be resolved at this level, we will advise on options such as Appeals.

Ensure Peace of Mind – While your problem resolution is in process you begin to feel better, knowing you are on your way. Then, with your problems behind, you can breathe easy and get on with your life.

> No more looking over your shoulder and worrying about the IRS! Life is good again thanks to Invictus Advisors.

What Else Can We Guarantee You? We guarantee that you'll always receive the personal attention that you deserve. Your tax problem is our highest priority. However, you must decide today that resolving your tax problem is your #1 priority. To get the process started visit invictus-advisors.com/taxproblems to get your FREE checklist.

Appendix

Figure 1.1

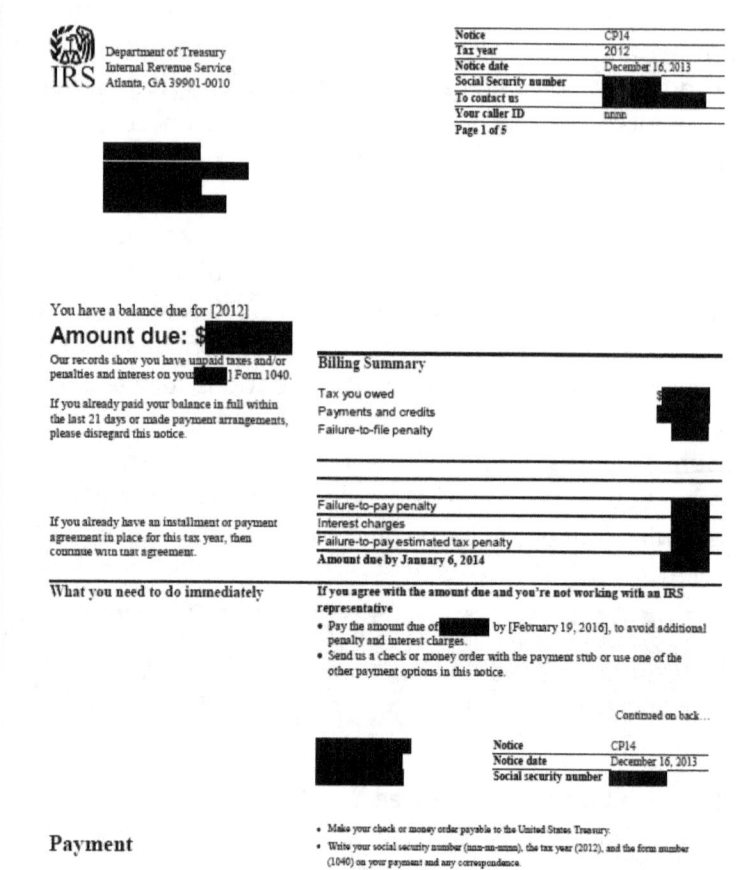

Figure 1.2

Department of the Treasury
Internal Revenue Service
Memphis, TN 38101-0069

IRS

7161 7618 3636 5326 0902

093811.395636.35206.1320 2 AT 0.384 1150

	SB
Notice	CP504
Tax Year	2003
Notice date	December 23, 2013
Social Security number	
To contact us	Phone 1-800-829-8374
Your Caller ID	583382
Page 1 of 4	

230869026101

053811

Notice of intent to levy
Intent to seize your property or rights to property
Amount due immediately: $14,467.08

As we notified you before, our records show you have unpaid taxes for the tax year ending December 31, 2003 (Form 1040). If you don't call us immediately or pay the amount due by January 2, 2014, we may seize ("levy") any state tax refund to which you're entitled and apply it to the $14,467.08 you owe.

If you still have an outstanding balance after we seize any state tax refund, we may take possession of your other property or your rights to property.

Billing Summary

Amount you owed	$14,392.36
Interest charges	74.72
Amount due immediately	$14,467.08

Continued on back...

IRS

Notice	CP504
Notice date	December 23, 2013
Social Security number	

Payment

- Make your check or money order payable to the United States Treasury.
- Write your Social Security number (   ), the tax year (2003), and the form number (1040) on your payment and any correspondence.

Amount due immediately	$14,467.08

INTERNAL REVENUE SERVICE
CINCINNATI, OH 45999-0150

HI   30 0 200312 670 0000000000

Figure 1.3

WI

IRS Department of the Treasury
Internal Revenue Service
ACS SUPPORT - STOP 5050
PO BOX 219236
KANSAS CITY, MO 64121-9236

7161761792845576523 8

Date:
NOV. 22, 2013

Taxpayer Identification Number:
Y 05

Case Reference Number:

Caller ID: 923879

Contact Telephone Number:
TOLL FREE: 1-800-829-7650
BEST ,TIME TO CALL:
MON - FRI   8:00 AM TO 8:00 PM LOCAL
ASISTENCIA EN ESPANOL 1-800-829-7650

RALEIGH   NC   27609-6314165

000211

CALL IMMEDIATELY TO PREVENT PROPERTY LOSS
FINAL NOTICE OF INTENT TO LEVY AND NOTICE OF YOUR RIGHT TO A HEARING

WHY WE ARE SENDING YOU THIS LETTER

We've written to you before asking you to contact us about your overdue taxes. You haven't responded or paid the amounts you owe. We encourage you to call us immediately at the telephone number listed above to discuss your options for paying these amounts. If you act promptly, we can resolve this matter without taking and selling your property to collect what you owe.

We are authorized to collect overdue taxes by taking, which is called levying, property or rights to property and selling them if necessary. Property includes bank accounts, wages, real estate commissions, business assets, cars and other income and assets.

WHAT YOU SHOULD DO

This is your notice, as required under Internal Revenue Code sections 6330 and 6331, that we intend to levy on your property or your rights to property 30 days after the date of this letter unless you take one of these actions:
- Pay the full amount you owe, shown on the back of this letter. When doing so,
    - Please make your check or money order payable to the United States Treasury;
    - Write your social security number and the tax year or employer identification number and the tax period on your payment; and enclose a copy of this letter with your payment.
- Make payment arrangements, such as an installment agreement that allows you to pay off your debt over time.
- Appeal the intended levy on your property by requesting a Collection Due Process hearing within 30 days from the date of this letter.

WHAT TO DO IF YOU DISAGREE

If you've paid already or think we haven't credited a payment to your account, please send us proof of that payment. You may also appeal our intended actions as described above.

Even if you request a hearing, please note that we can still file a Notice of Federal Tax Lien at any time to protect the government's interest. A lien is a public notice that tells your creditors that the government has a right to your current assets and any assets you acquire after we file the lien.

We've enclosed two publications that explain how we collect past due taxes and your collection appeal rights, as required under Internal Revenue Code sections 6330 and 6331. In addition, we've enclosed a form that you can use to request a Collection Due Process hearing.

We look forward to hearing from you immediately, and hope to assist you in fulfilling your responsibility as a taxpayer.

Enclosures: Copy of letter, Form 12153, Publication 594, Publication 1660, Envelope

243882292103

Automated Collection System

Letter 1058 (Rev. 05-2002)(LT-11)

Figure 1.4

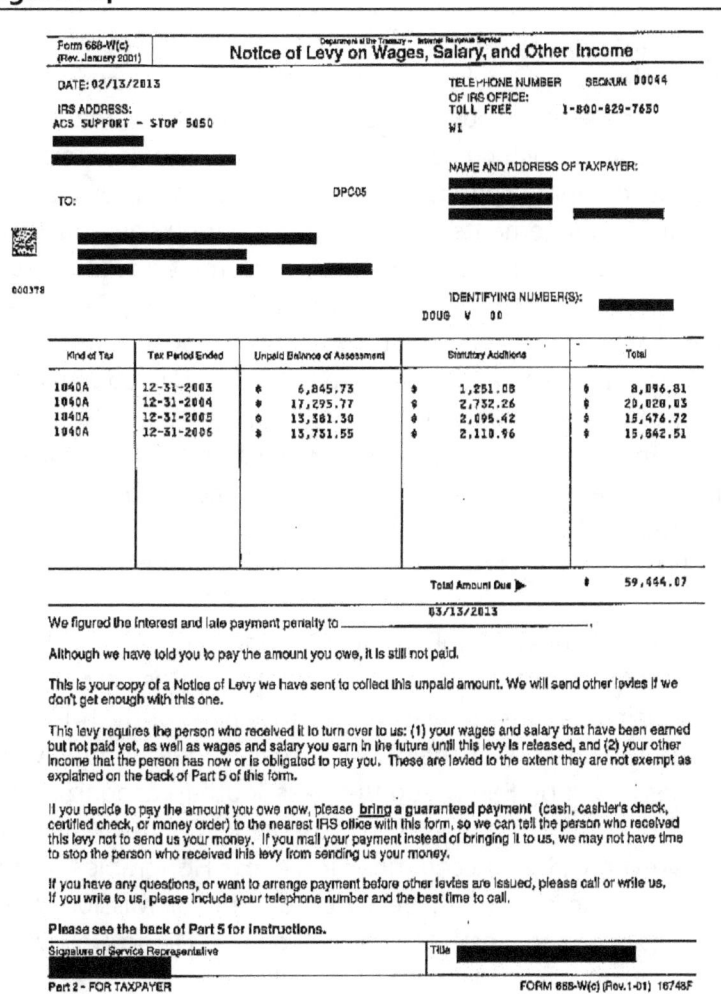

About Vidal Espinosa

Vidal Espinosa, MBA is very involved with the local business community. He co-founded Invictus Advisors Foundation a non-profit 501 (c) 3 whose mission is to provide new business owners and start-up businesses relief from financial, marketing, and personal coaching obligations to position their enterprises to grow to their full potential. Additionally he has provided free speaking engagements to members of various organizations such as the National City Chamber of Commerce, Masters in Networking (a small business networking group), Otay Mesa Chamber of Commerce, Accion – San Diego (a non-profit business lender) and the Greater San Diego Business Association. Vidal has done work with Auntie Helen's (providing over $10,000 in-kind audit work), reduced rates for Moderate Majority (a veteran's organization), and sponsored the University of San Diego School of Law/Procopio International Tax Institute 2015.

His most recent accomplishments include: Finalist as the CFO of the Year Awards 2016 by San Diego Business Journal recognizing San Diego financial professionals for the roles they play in the success of their businesses ; Top Minority Owned Business 2015 by San Diego Business Journal recognizing top minority-owned businesses in San Diego County ranked by gross revenue; Best Accounting Firm - 2015 Honorable Mention by San Diego City Beat; Best Accountant for Mission Valley News (2015) and Best Accountant for San Diego Downtown News (2016).

About Invictus Advisors

In the accounting, tax and business consulting field there seems to be a way to make it to the top and become a forefront industry specialist. Invictus Advisors has done that, in San Diego, California and beyond. Countless clients in various industries turn to us for a host of special services, and their record of delivery has surpassed many of our competitors.

The expert knowledge that Invictus Advisors offers clients translates to a winning combination. So when a company is looking for accounting, business consulting or tax assistance, they will find Invictus Advisors is poised to meet their needs. Bilingual service is yet another advantage securing them as a proactive problem-solving team of professionals.

The wide array of skills that the partners have picked up is of particular pride. They are equipped to help small and large businesses to meet their organizational goals and legal obligations. Some things are inescapable, such as taxes. Organizations without internal personnel to handle this are flocking to Invictus for help.

- Vidal Espinosa holds an MBA and a CPA in Mexico, so clients can put his education and experience to work on their behalf. He also has a background with large firms and a professorship to his credit. Budgets, cash forecasting, audits at various levels, tax advising, business start-up requirements and so much more are the assets he brings to clients.

- Jeff Redondo is marketing and business development savvy. He holds a Bachelor's degree, certificates in Fund Raising Management and Non-profit Management. Training and procedure development for businesses are some of his strengths.

When clients secure Vidal and Jeff as part of their business enhancement strategy, they gain the full measure of skills and knowledge they've gleaned through study and experience.

One stand-out service they offer at Invictus Advisors is the free, no obligation meetings, where it's possible to discuss the special approach that will work to fill their needs. During that 20-minute meeting, they provide a financial answer to businesses' owners most pressing problems and give away three business building strategies. If the potential client is not satisfied with the value of the free meeting, Invictus Advisors will donate $100 to the person's charity of choice.

Another feature they possess to excel in the marketplace is our fixed fees systems. This means clients are not nickel and dimed for every little part. Invictus Advisors have also invested their own capital in what we believe to be an outlier sales marketing system which every client is eligible to use.

This is one of many examples of how they make clients' needs a top priority. Invictus works with clients and places a strong emphasis on relationships. They have come up with so many solutions that free up client time, something known as task time reduction. Essentially, their savvy becomes that of the clients; because their heart is for their clients. Their desire is to see their clients grow, thrive and become optimally successful in their chosen industry.

Their website is flooded with testimonials from clients in the insurance industry, craft importers, auto body shops, nurseries, hair care industry providers, loan services and insurance services.

Patricia D. shared how their business saved over $10,000 in taxes after securing the services of Invictus Advisors. *"They have given me the flexibility to grow my business instead of worrying about planning my tax situation. My partner and I are amazed at the quality and expertise of their team,"* she stated.

> **For more information, visit**
> **http://www.invictus-advisors.com/**

www.ingramcontent.com/pod-product-compliance
Lightning Source LLC
Chambersburg PA
CBHW070411190526
45169CB00003B/1206